SOCIAL MEDIA
CONTENT TO CASH

EASILY CREATE CONTENT FOR SOCIAL MEDIA
(AND MAKE MONEY FROM YOUR CONTENT)

SOCIAL MEDIA CONTENT TO CASH

Easily Create Content for Social Media (And Make Money from Your Content)

Startup Jahswill

Table of Contents

Introduction

For those of you who don't know me, my name is StartUP Jahswill. I'm a small business expert and Digital Marketer. I am not a guru. I'm just like you. I have businesses that run online and offline.

Over the past 12 years, I have started over 10 businesses with varying degrees of success. I have written several books, one of them is published on Amazon. I have also helped many business owners to start and grow their businesses as part of my consulting business.

In my personal experience as a business person and with many businesses that I have worked with, I have noticed that leveraging the internet is a great way to easily grow your business. However, many business owners don't know how to successfully take a business online.

That is why I created the Facebook group "Take Your Business Online". The goal is to take 1,000 businesses online by end of year 2020. If you are not a member of that group, you should join it. Here is the link to join the "Take Your Busines Online" Facebook group.

From the feedback I have received so far, it has been an amazing success journey. Still, I have also noticed that many who sell online struggle with the number one thing that drives sales and grow your business online - CONTENT!

You see the basic secret to making money whether that is offline or online is to offer value. To solve problems that people have.

People do not buy THINGS; they buy the VALUE (SOLUTION) that the things offer.

You buy a phone, it's because it solves a problem. Maybe it's a communication problem, or the problem of capturing and keeping memories alive. Otherwise, we will still be using a Nokia 3310 today.

People buy clothes not just for covering nakedness, but also for prestige, class, etc.

You must understand this concept if you want to make money.

The thing is if you can offer massive amount of VALUE (SOLUTION) to a huge number of people, you are sure to make it online.

So, whatever you are selling online (products or services) think of it as a VALUE provider, a SOLUTION provider. Knowing this will help you understand the concept of CONTENT 2 CASH.

You will use your CONTENT to provide VALUE and get CASH in return.

People go online for one and one reason alone - CONTENT.

When they open Google, they are searching for content with answers to their questions.

When they open Facebook, they are searching for content about their friends and to express themslves.

When they login to Instagram, they are searching for amazing picture content.

Content drives the internet. The internet was actually created because of content. As a means of organizing content and making it available for anyone, anywhere. That's why content is everything. Some people even say Content is King!

If you have anything to sell online, you must have the ability to create compelling content that pulls in customers and sales. Getting paid for creating quality content should be one of your goals online.

This guide is designed to help you achieve just that: Converting content to cash online.

What you'll learn

Learn how to easily create content posts

Discover how to easily come up with content ideas

How to legally 'steal' and use other people's content

Discover what type of content you should be posting

Learn the best time to post so that more people can see your posts (this is GOLD!)

Discover the tools that the Pros use to easily create content

Discover how to never stress your head again to create content (I will show a content resource that if you choose to, you'll never ever create content again, just use already-made content!) - Please don't share this with anyone.

Learn how to create content that sells

Who is this guide for?

Anyone who has anything to sell online

Social media managers who help other businesses to manage their social media

Business owners who want to take their businesses online

Before we go in deep, let's understand what content is.

Part 1

What is Content?

According to wikipedia "content is the information and experiences that are directed toward an end-user or audience"

Another important thing about content, especially when it

comes to professional content writing, is the value that you deliver. Unless your content is useful to the readers, it is not going to be useful to you or your brand.

Content comes in any form (audio, text, video)

Content Types:

1. Written posts, blogs, articles, guides

2. Electronic books (eBooks)

3. Links to external content

4. Images

5. Videos

6. Video Stories

7. Live Videos

8. Infographics

9. Testimonials and reviews

10. Podcasts

Part 2

Why You Should Create Content

As I mentioned earlier, content is what people come online for. So, if you create valuable content that people want to see, they will naturally flock to you like flies to shit.

The following are some very good reasons why you may create content:

- Increase brand awareness

- Build relationships

- Gain valuable customer data

- Improve search ranking

- Increase website traffic

- Increase customer's loyalty to you brand

- Improve customer service

- Cheaper and targeted advertisement

- Helps to build global business

- Enables measuring the effectiveness of online campaigns

Generally, any type of content will do one or more of the following:

- Educate

- Entertain

- Inspire

- Promote

Educational content teaches the audience and guides them to reliable information. Like the one you are receiving now.

Entertaining content relieves stress and makes your audience drawn closer to you as they see your human side. Like jokes, comedy and songs.

Inspirational content sparks your audience thinking and motivates them to do greater things. Riddles and motivational quotes are some examples.

Promotional content encourages your audience to buy whatever you are selling. When you post about what you are selling or how good your product and customer service is you are promoting. Or when you ask people to buy your products, this is promotional content.

As a business owner online who wants to sell, your goal is to find a good mix of content that achieves all.

The most important content type is the one that educates. This type of content builds trust and authority among your ideal customers.

If you are to succeed on social media, you must create at least 3 of this type of content. Namely: educational, entertaining and promotional.

One common mistake many people make on social media is creating only promotional content. They forget that social media is what it is: social website!

People don't open Facebook or Instagram for the purpose of looking for what to buy. They want entertainment, trending news, gossips etc.

The only reason social media is a powerful tool for selling is because many people gather there. It's just like a sports stadium, people gather there to watch sports. However, a lot of selling happen there because of the number people there. As they are watching football, they will need water, Ice-cream, team paraphernalia, etc.

But sports stadia are not marketplaces per se. therefore, if you go to a stadium to watch a football match and all you see are people selling stuff and not football players, you are not going to be happy. You will quickly leave.

That is just how people who see your constant promotional content will likely react on social media. Get bored, angry and disappointed.

That is one mistake you must avoid if you want to convert Content to Cash.

In my book, Facebook Marketing Mistakes that are Holding Your Business Down, I identified 14 other such mistakes you need to avoid if you must succeed abundantly on Facebook.

You can get a copy at a special discount by clicking here.

Let's continue.

Now that you realize how important content is and that you must create content that your customers want to see, what type of content should you create?

Let me show you:

Part 3

What Type of Content Should You Create?

The content you create must be useful. Useful to your customer by meeting anyone of the needs we mentioned earlier.

Information that is useful has a context, easy to consume, shareable and non intrusive.

You also want to create content that your customers will like, comment on and share. This way you can increase your potential reach.

What Motivates Users to Share Content?

There is proven science behind what motivates users to share content online. Different researches have discovered psychological triggers that motivate people to engage in online activities.

Here are some of the most important ones:

Social Approval: People love to be loved. They express their personality hoping to receive positive feedback from their circle of friends and acquaintances. People share content to express their personality on social groups.

Communication: Humans are social animals. They want to build relationships with other people, and online content enables humans to do this more easily and frequently.

Support Ideas: People also use social media to signal support for ideas, political views and personal beliefs. In this is way they are able to relate with something of greater good.

Entertainment: When you come to think of it many people use social media to wind down. At least I know I do and so does my wife. This type of content includes memes, comedy skits, humor, videos, music, and more.

Focus on content that adds value to the reader's life. It can add value by making them smarter, making them laugh, making them do their job better, rush to their child to share the video, make a contribution to a charity.

You must understand that the value of any content differs from person to person.

What is of high value to one may be of no value to another. Just because something is of high value to you does not make it high-value content. There is a saying that "an old woman does not laugh when they mention dry bones". Thus, you must ensure that the content you create resonates with your audience, your target customer.

Imagine a business that sells products (say body lotion) to people with albinism sharing sarcastic jokes about albinos! Do you think his target audience will find the joke funny? (Oh by the way, I think this is a great business idea, developing special natural body lotion for people with albinism, I have never seen any adverts for such a product.)

High-value content is about your audience; it is not about you. Your content should speak to your audience. Speak to their needs, problems, and pain-points.

How do you then find out what your target audience wants to see?

1. Use your analytics

Facebook analytics is one of the best ways to find out what your audience likes. Your social media analytics can reveal what's working and what's not.

The interesting thing is that Facebook has a free tool called Audience Insight which you can use. By studying your top-performing posts, you can quickly tell what is resonating with your audience. Your job is to find these posts and re-create them or something similar.

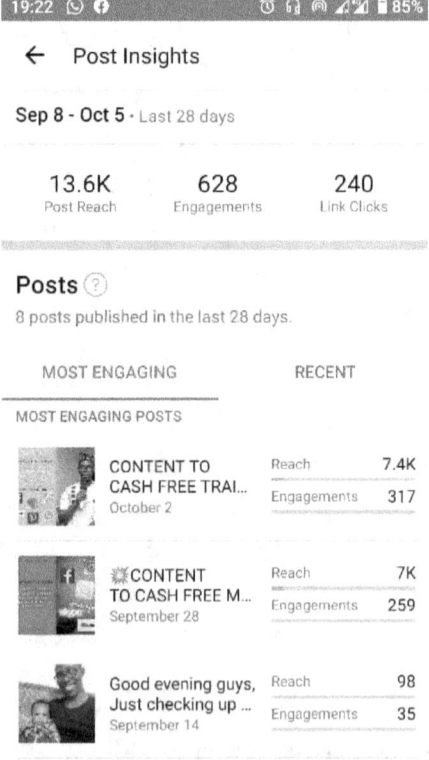

2. Ask your audience

The second strategy is to ask your audience.

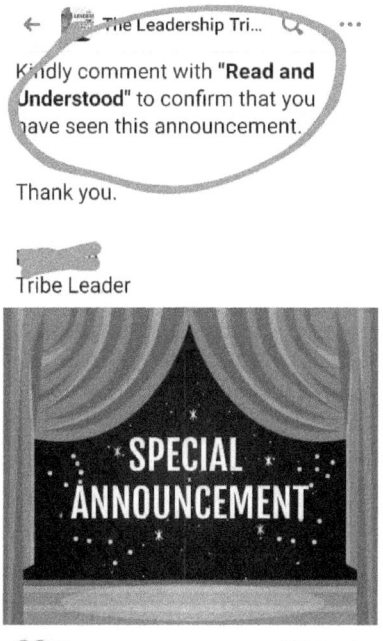

You could simply ask a question to your followers or use a poll on your social media page. For example, "What type of content do you want to see us sharing more?" "What skill do you want me to teach for free here?" and so on.

3. Learn from your industry peers

The third strategy is to learn from your industry peers.

Look at the top pages in your industry and see what is working for them. Since your target customers is likely going to be similar to theirs, what worked for them will likely work for you too.

It'll be great to go beyond just your competitors. Are there other companies that you admire, which you can learn from?

4. Use a research tool

Another strategy is to use a social media content research tool such as Buzzsumo.

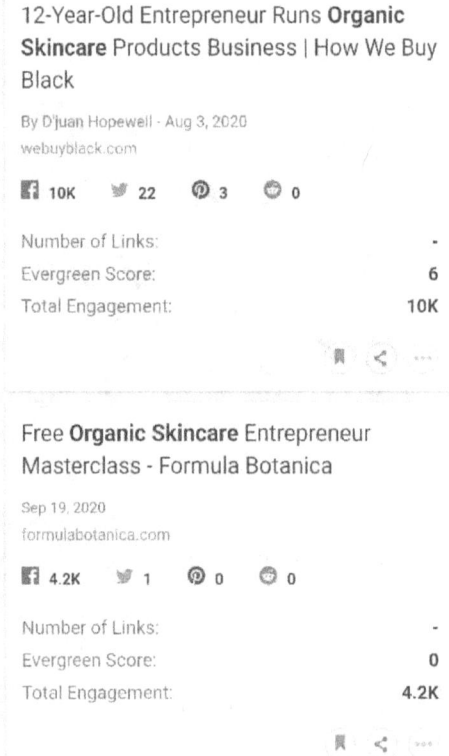

12-Year-Old Entrepreneur Runs **Organic Skincare** Products Business | How We Buy Black

By D'juan Hopewell · Aug 3, 2020
webuyblack.com

f 10K   🐦 22   📌 3   ⊙ 0

Number of Links: -
Evergreen Score: 6
Total Engagement: 10K

Free **Organic Skincare** Entrepreneur Masterclass - Formula Botanica

Sep 19, 2020
formulabotanica.com

f 4.2K   🐦 1   📌 0   ⊙ 0

Number of Links: -
Evergreen Score: 0
Total Engagement: 4.2K

Buzzsumo is the social media version of Google for the most shared content. You can search for any keywords (say "organic skincare"), and Buzzsumo will show you the most shared content that's relevant to the keyword.

5. Create buyer personas

A buyer persona is a profile of your ideal customer complete with their demographics, behaiviours and interests. The fifth strategy is to create buyer personas. Your buyer personas will give you ideas on what content to create and share on social media.

In this video (https://www.youtube.com/watch?v=oQacYq7RWDM), I explain how you can use Facebook to easily create your buyer persona. You can watch it later at the end of this class.

6. Follow trends

Finally, you should keep an eye out for general trends in the social media space and follow them. This will help you get a general sense of the types of content to post. While it won't be very specific to your audience, I think it can still be helpful.

Part 4

How to Easily Come Up With Valuable Content

1. Use the World Wide Web

First off, visit websites and blogs that publish content you love and know your audience will love too. Whether that's visual content on Pinterest or editorial content on Newspapers, make a habit of regularly visiting reliable sources of content that excites you.

Read through the comments and follow links in articles that catch your attention, and do some digging. You should focus on content that works for your own content strategy, and make a note of any related links, sentences, or ideas that might help you.

2. Listen, Watch, and Learn from Leaders

Follow leader who inspire you. Subscribe to their blogs and social profiles, and read their stories. These people could be influencers in your industry, or they could just as easily be bold figures in other areas of your life that you admire.

3. Transform Existing Content

When you finally find that wonderful idea, explore it. Shake it around, and turn it inside out. Don't be afraid to make it into something new.

There are several ways to do this:

- Combine two completely different ideas into one

- You could translate ideas from one format to another

- Think of alternative ways you can make use of the original content

4. 'Steal' it from your Competitors

All businesses eye their competition and study them for insights.. You should not be afraid to do it too. Copy their ideas and put them in your own words.

Wikipedia also says "Content also leads to influencing other people in creating their own content, sometimes in a way that the original author did not or could not plan or imagine. This feature, adding the option of user innovation in a medium, means that users can develop their own content from existing content. Much social media content is derived in this way, by effectively re-cycling content in a slightly different format."

This is the easiest way to create your own content without much stress and too much thinking. Just copy, edit in your own words and booooom! Your post is ready.

Amateurs wait for inspiration, professionals spy on their competition.

I think it was the famous world-renown artist Pablo Picasso who said "Good artists borrow, great artists steal". You can actually legally steal other people's content in this way without getting caught.

It's a secret that the pros have employed for years. Copy,

Edit, Publish, Own.

Nothing is really new in this world; we are just saying the same thing in different ways or doing the same things in different ways.

5. Industry Thought Leaders

This is more than a competitive analysis and straight to the organizations and associations that create thought leadership that can sometimes determine the direction of your business.

Take their content and make it your own by transforming it.

6. Social media and trending topics

- Facebook's saved posts

- Twitter lists

- Pinterest boards

- Whatsapp groups

- Quora

- Nairaland

BBNaija, death of public figure, celebrity gossip etc. Just be careful to make sure that what and how you are positioning this content resonates with your audience and your overall content goal.

7. Repurpose your content

The same piece of content that you create can be converted

to different format and use multiple times.

You wrote a text post on Facebook? Use the information to record a short video and post on Instagram stories. Extract the audio alone from the video and post. Screenshot the text on Facebook and post it as a picture on Instagram. Use same information to record a longer video and post on Youtube and Facebook.

This is another gem you want to take away from this training. Getting new ideas may not come easy, but reusing what you already have is very easy.

One piece of content = multiple pieces of content!

8. Share content from other sources

If you come across a good piece of content that your audience may benefit from and you don't want to "steal" it by reverse-engineering, then just click the share button and share to your page.

For inspiration, here are 30 content ideas you can create and post for every day of the month:

1. Share Positive Statistics and News

2. Share and Repurpose User-Generated Content

4. Campaign for Social Causes

Social causes connect really well with people. Everyone wants to contribute to social causes in some way or the other.

5. Take a picture of your workspace

6. Answer a question

7. Introduce your newest products on social media

8. Interview a customer

9. Interview an influencer

10. Share something about a community event you're looking forward to

11. Post about a training or seminar you are attending

12. Share something funny

13. Share your business story

Every business and organization has a story — some longer than others. Look for opportunities to share pieces of that story to let people know why you do what you do.

14. Share someone else's post

15. Post a #TBT, #MotivationMonday

16. Post something about the season

17. Share some inspirational and motivational quotes

18. Spotlight a customer of the month

19. Share an attention-grabbing statistic

20. Ask a multiple choice question (may be a poll)

21. Create a video, featuring people or products from your business

22. Share a link to an article

23. Correct a common misconception that people in your business industry can relate to

24. Post a list of your favorite thought-leaders

25. Share your favorite book or playlist

26. Give a shout out to a friend or partner business

27. Show off your skills and knowledge by sharing posts about it.

28. Post something in celebration of a business milestone achieved

29. Cross-promote your social networks

30. Thank your customers for their support

You can use this to form a content calendar for your business. Post each of these ideas from 1st to 30th, and then repeat the process the following month.

Part 5

When to Post Your Content

Is there even anything like a 'best time to post on Facebook?' The short answer is Yes! The long answer: the best time to post on Facebook depends on your followers and when they're mostly active online. However, there are a few general trends to keep in mind when timing your posts.

Posting when your target audience is online will

increase the likelihood of them seeing your post and therefore are more likely to click like or comment. When your posts receive a lot of engagement, Facebook's new algorithm will prioritize content from your brand and place it at the top of users' feeds.

With the growing complexity of Facebook's ever-changing algorithm, finding the best time to post on Facebook is more difficult every year.

But it's still worth researching—the truth is, the right time for you to post on Facebook will be different from the right time for someone else to post on Facebook.

I'll show you some general patterns you can use to get started, and I'll offer strategies to help you find the best time to post on Facebook for your business.

Let's talk about the general patterns.

According to a research by HubSpot, the best day to post on Facebook for a high click-through rate is Sunday. There is no significant difference between weekdays, but there is a slight dip in clicks on Fridays and Saturdays.

Hootsuite conducted research and found a difference in the best day for B2B and B2C companies to post content. According to the research Monday and Tuesday are the best days for B2B businesses, and Tuesday is the best day for B2C companies.

Hootsuite's research also showed that the best time to post on Facebook for B2C brands is around noon, corresponding with lunchtime when many people are on a break from work. If you are a B2B company, the best time to post on

Facebook is any point during standard work hours, especially from 9 a.m. to 2 p.m.

Now, how can you determine the best time for YOU to post for maximum engagement?

By reviewing post analytics and researching user activity, you can find out when your audience is on Facebook and likely to engage with your content.

Strategy Number 1: Use Facebook Analytics

The first and possibly the most effective way is to look at your posts and audience insights on Facebook.

You can also use Facebook analytics (Insights) to get an overview of when your audience is mostly active, helping you to determine when might be the best time for you to post on Facebook.

Strategy Number 2: Test, Test and Test

Another way to determine when your target audience is the most engaged is to post the same content at different times. This gives you a way to see how your content perform based on when you post.

Strategy Number 3: Perform a Competitor Analysis

Follow competitors' Facebook business pages to track how they're timing their posts so you're able to improve your own scheduling.

Compare your competitors' posting schedule to your audience yours. Are there sme times when your audience is active, but your competitors don't typically post?

Scheduling your content to go out at those times can help you stand out and have less competition for post engagement.

Well, now it's clear: the best times to post on Facebook—along with Twitter and Instagram, for that matter—depend on your specific audience and their social media habits.

Part 6

How Often Should You Post on Social Media?

This will depend largely on your audience size, audience needs, variety of post and a few other things. Remember, what works for one business may not work for another.

So, instead of focusing on how often, focus on these proven strategies:

- •Post consistently - show up every day and show up strong

- •Post quality and valuable content

- •Be objective and goal-oriented with every single post

- •Engage with your audience regularly

- •Post variety of content types

As a general rule though, you can use the following

template to guide your posting schedule:

Facebook 1 - 3 times per day

Instagram 2 - 5 times per day

Twitter 3 -10 times per day

Pinterest 3 - 5 times per day

Youtube 1 video weekly

Bonus

Some Tools for Creating Social Media Content

Here is a list of my favorite visual marketing tools:

Phone – my pocket office

Canva - Create Infographics, images, etc. (https://www.canva.com/join/loop-candy-protective)

OBS – Record screen and video lessons

Whatsapp - saving ideas for later use.

Bonus 1

Plan Campaigns

These can be around:

- Campaigns to promote events.

- A series of posts promoting a single piece of content.

- A set of branded posts carrying a consistent message or hashtag.

At this point I know your blood is already pumping fast! You can't wait to start putting these ideas into practice.

You see, if you can strategically implement the ideas covered in this free training you will easily convert content to cash on the internet. I really hope that you will act immediately while the ideas are still fresh and start making cool money on the internet with your content. I want you to actually act on them.

That is the reason why I have written 3 guides that will serve as a roadmap for you to implement these ideas easily and start making money on Facebook.

The guides are very easy to consume and implement. They are actionable and very short and straight to the point.

All 3 guides are part of the **Facebook Business Success Series Kit** – a complete package of EVERYTHING you need to know to use content to make money on Facebook successfully.

The guides will easily blow your business on Facebook and make you thousands if not millions

They are:

1. Facebook for Business Success - *Top Secrets to Help You Run a Successful Business on Facebook*

2. Facebook Posts Engagement Secrets: *20 Proven Strategies to Get More Likes, Comments and Shares on Your Facebook Posts*

3. Facebook Marketing Mistakes: *14 Newbies Mistakes that are Holding Your business Down*

If you have these 3 guides with this imformation you just received in this training today, your money business on Facebook is covered.

My-Word-is-My-Bond Money-Back Guarantee

The other sweet thing is that if after 180days you have religiously followed ALL the methods, tricks and ideas that I will share with you and you have not made your first cash from content, then I will refund you the money you paid for the 3 guides.

Yes, just tell me that you don't want to do again and I will refund your money 100%. And you will still get to keep the guides.

If this is not a no-brainer I don't know what is!

Get the 3 guides now and be on your way to converting content to cash.

Paystack Payment (Nigerians):

All 3
https://paystack.com/pay/complete-facebook-business-series-special-offer

Any 2 of the books

Book A

Book B

Book C

Business Plan Book:

(https://paystack.com/buy/no-bullshit-business-plan-how-to-write-a-business-plan-easil)

Flutterwave Payment (Internationals):

All 3

Any 2

Book A

Book B

Book C

Business Plan Book:
(https://flutterwave.com/store/startupcrest/xaehwok13jvs)

About the Author

StartUP Jahswill

Entrepreneur | Public Speaker | Business Coach

Eduzobe Jahswill Udogbo (StartUP Jahswill) is a trained Physicist with a passion for building and growing small businesses.

He is the CEO of StartUP Crest, a company he formed to help young people start and grow small businesses. He is also the CEO of LabHub Medical Laboratories and Diagnostics and the founding Managing Partner/General Manager of Karone Photo World Ltd, both very successful startups.

In 2009 he setup his first registered company, SwiftTech Integrated Solutions Ltd with the aim of providing alternative power supply to residents of the satellite towns around the Nigerian capital territory, Abuja.

Although that venture turned out to be a total failure, Jahswill learned valuable lessons that have helped him to start and grow other businesses with varied degrees of success.

His number one desire is to help as many young people as possible to discover their entrepreneurial skills and use this to start and grow businesses that will provide employment and livelihood.

His mission is simple: help young people transition from frustrated job seekers and disillusioned startups to successful entrepreneurs.

He promotes financial education that helps young people understand the career options available to them as a means of creating wealth as opposed to the old one-way thinking of "Go to School, get a good job and live comfortably ever after"!

Jahswill appreciates that while university/college education might be a necessity in some chosen careers, it is just one of the options and not the surest path to creating wealth. That is why he advocates learning business and financial skills that gives the best and surest path to wealth creation. He spends most of his time developing content for his various educational platforms especially his blog www.startupcrest.com where he provides valuable resources for startups.

He is happily married and blessed with a beautiful daughter.